DATE DUE

NO 18 '94			
MR 12 '98			
DE 7 '98			
NO 9 '99			
DE 3 '99			
DE 9 '03			
MR 28 '06		56	
AP 7 '06		18	
JA 6 '07		74	

DEMCO 38-296

PIANO / VOCAL / GUITAR

THE GERSHWIN ·COLLECTION·

ISBN 0-7935-1337-5

 Hal Leonard Publishing Corporation

THE GERSHWIN COLLECTION

▪ C O L L E C T I O N ▪

BESS, YOU IS MY WOMAN

(From "PORGY AND BESS")

Words by DUBOSE HEYWARD & IRA GERSHW[IN]
Music by GEORGE GERSHW[IN]

BIDIN' MY TIME

Words by IRA GERSHWIN
Music by GEORGE GERSHWIN

Moderato

Gracefully

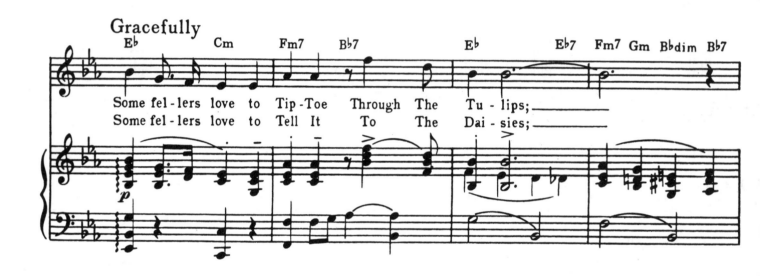

Some fel-lers love to Tip-Toe Through The Tu - lips;
Some fel-lers love to Tell It To The Dai - sies;

Some fel-lers go on Sing - ing In The Rain.
Some Stroll Be-neath The Hon - ey-suc-kle Vines;

BUT NOT FOR ME

Words by IRA GERSHWIN
Music by GEORGE GERSHWIN

19

BY STRAUSS

Words by IRA GERSHWIN
Music by GEORGE GERSHWIN

Tempo di Valse Viennoise

A - way with the mu - sic of Broad - way! ____ Be off with your Irv - ing Ber - lin! ____

*Written for "The Show Is On" (1936)

EMBRACEABLE YOU

Words by IRA GERSHWIN
Music by GEORGE GERSHWIN

Doz-ens of girls would storm__ up; I had to lock my door. Some-how I could-n't warm__ up to one be-fore.

What was it that con-trolled__ me? What kept my love life lean? My in-tu-i-tion told__

CLAP YO' HANDS

Words by IRA GERSHWIN
Music by GEORGE GERSHWIN

DO, DO, DO

Words by IRA GERSHWIN
Music by GEORGE GERSHWIN

Moderato grazioso

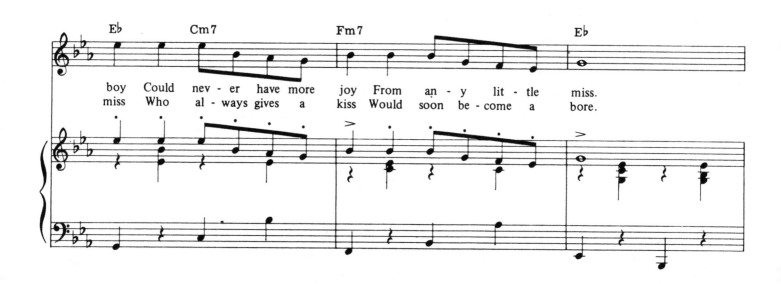

FASCINATING RHYTHM

Words by IRA GERSHWIN
Music by GEORGE GERSHWIN

A FOGGY DAY
(From "A DAMSEL IN DISTRESS")

Words by IRA GERSHW
Music by GEORGE GERSHW

FOR YOU, FOR ME, FOR EVERMORE

Words by IRA GERSHWIN
Music by GEORGE GERSHWIN

HOW LONG HAS THIS BEEN GOING ON?

Words by IRA GERSHWIN
Music by GEORGE GERSHWIN

He: As a tot, when I trot-ted in lit-tle vel-vet pant ies, ___
She: 'Neath the stars at ba-zaars of-ten I've had to ca-ress men, ___

I was kissed by my sis-ters, my cous-ins and my aunt-ies. ___
Five or ten dol-lars then I'd col-lect from all those yes-men. ___

Sad to tell, it was Hell, an in-fer-no worse than Dan-te's. ___
Don't be sad, I must add that they meant no more than chess-men. ___

I GOT PLENTY O' NUTTIN'
(From "PORGY AND BESS")

Words by IRA GERSHWIN and DuBOSE HEYWA
Music by GEORGE GERSHW

I GOT RHYTHM
(From "GIRL CRAZY")

Words by IRA GERSHWIN
Music by GEORGE GERSHWIN

I LOVE TO RHYME

Words by IRA GERSHWIN
Music by GEORGE GERSHWIN

I'VE GOT A CRUSH ON YOU

Words by IRA GERSHWIN
Music by GEORGE GERSHWIN

wore down my re-sist-ance: I fell, _____ and it was swell. _____

She: You're my big and brave and hand-some Ro-me-o. How I

won you I shall nev-er, nev-er know. *He:* It's not that you're at-trac-tive, But

IT AIN'T NECESSARILY SO

(From "PORGY AND BESS")

Words by IRA GERSHW
Music by GEORGE GERSHW

LET'S CALL THE WHOLE THING OFF

Words by IRA GERSHWIN
Music by GEORGE GERSHWIN

LIZA
(ALL THE CLOUDS'LL ROLL AWAY)

Words by GUS KAHN and IRA GERSHWIN
Music by GEORGE GERSHWIN

LOVE IS HERE TO STAY

(From "GOLDWYN FOLLIES")

Words by IRA GERSHW
Music by GEORGE GERSHW

LOVE IS SWEEPING THE COUNTRY

Words by IRA GERSHWIN
Music by GEORGE GERSHWIN

LOVE WALKED IN

Words by IRA GERSHWIN
Music by GEORGE GERSHWIN

THE MAN I LOVE

Words by IRA GERSHWIN
Music by GEORGE GERSHWIN

MY MAN'S GONE NOW
(From "PORGY AND BESS")

Words by DuBOSE HEYWARD
Music by GEORGE GERSHWIN

NICE WORK IF YOU CAN GET IT
(From "A DAMSEL IN DISTRESS")

Words by IRA GERSHWIN
Music by GEORGE GERSHWIN

Moderato

The man who on-ly lives for mak-ing mon-ey   Lives a life that is-n't

nec-es-sa-ri-ly sun-ny.   Like-wise the man who works for fame,

There's no guar-an-tee that time won't e-rase his name.

OF THEE I SING

Words by IRA GERSHWIN
Music by GEORGE GERSHWIN

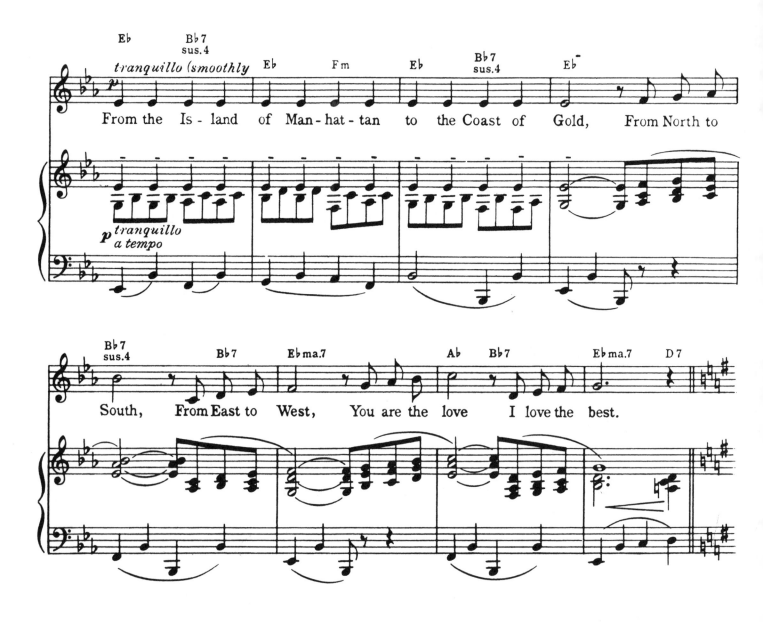

From the Is - land of Man - hat - tan to the Coast of Gold, From North to South, From East to West, You are the love I love the best.

OH, LADY BE GOOD!

Words By
IRA GERSHWIN

Words by IRA GERSHWIN
Music by GEORGE GERSHWIN

OH LAWD, I'M ON MY WAY
(From "PORGY AND BESS")

Words by IRA GERSHWIN and DuBOSE HEYWARD
Music by GEORGE GERSHWIN

THE REAL AMERICAN FOLK SONG
(IS A RAG)

Words by IRA GERSHWIN
Music by GEORGE GERSHWIN

Written for "Ladies First" (1918)
The first George and Ira Gershwin collaboration used in a Broadway show

SLAP THAT BASS

Words by IRA GERSHWIN
Music by GEORGE GERSHWIN

'S WONDERFUL
(From "FUNNY FACE")

Words by IRA GERSHWIN
Music by GEORGE GERSHWIN

SHALL WE DANCE

Words by IRA GERSHWIN
Music by GEORGE GERSHWIN

Drop— that long face!— Come on, have— your fling!

Why— keep nurs-ing— the Blues?———

134

SOMEBODY LOVES ME

(From "SHE LOVES ME")

Words by BALLARD MacDONALD and B.G. DeSYL
Music by GEORGE GERSHW

SOMEONE TO WATCH OVER ME

(From "OH KAY!")

Words by IRA GERSHWIN
Music by GEORGE GERSHWIN

There's a say-ing old Says that love is blind, Still we're of-ten told "Seek and
Un pro-ver-be dit l'a-mour a-veu-glé, On nous dit aus-si: "Cher-chez

ye shall find". So I'm going to seek A cer-tain lad I've had in mind.
pour trou-ver" Je cher-che ce gail-lard qui m'est res-té dans l'i-dée

REFRAIN

a tempo

There's a some bod-y I'm long-ing to see. I hope that he Turns out to be
Il est un quel-qu'un que je veux re-voir Cha-que ma-tin et cha-que soir,

Some-one who'll watch o-ver me._____ I'm a lit-tle lamb who's
Et qui me pro té-ge - ra._____ Je suis la bre - bis per -

lost in the wood. I know I could Al-ways be good To one who'll
due dans le bois. Je don - ne-rai Tou-te ma foi A qui me

watch o-ver me._____ Al-though he may not be the
pro - té-ge - ra._____ Quoi - qu'il ne soit pas un hom -

STRIKE UP THE BAND

Words by IRA GERSHWIN
Music by GEORGE GERSHWIN

SUMMERTIME

(From "PORGY AND BESS")

Words by DuBOSE HEYWAR[D]
Music by GEORGE GERSHW[IN]

Allegretto semplice

mf espr.

p

mp

R.H.

Moderato (with expressio[n])

Am6 E7

Sum - mer - time

tranquillo

8va

p

pp *molto legato*

Am6 E7 Am6 E7 Am6 E7 Am6

— an' the liv - in' is eas - y, Fish are

Dm F6 Dm7 Fmaj7 D#dim E B7(#9)

jump - in' an' the cot - ton is high.

poco rit.

mf *a tempo*

SWANEE

Words by IRVING CAESAR
Music by GEORGE GERSHWIN

THEY ALL LAUGHED

Words by IRA GERSHWIN
Music by GEORGE GERSHWIN

THEY CAN'T TAKE THAT AWAY FROM ME

Words by IRA GERSHWIN
Music by GEORGE GERSHWIN

A WOMAN IS A SOMETIME THING
(From "PORGY AND BESS")

Words by DuBOSE HEYWARD
Music by GEORGE GERSHWIN